CW00344324

ANN GRIFFITHS

THE FURNACE AND THE FOUNTAIN

Ann Griffiths

The Furnace and the Fountain

A.M. ALLCHIN

CARDIFF
UNIVERSITY OF WALES PRESS
1987

First edition 1987
Reprinted 1990

© University of Wales and the Welsh Arts Council 1987

British Library Cataloguing in Publication Data

Allchin, A.M.
  Ann Griffiths   The Furnace and the Fountain
  1. Griffiths, Ann, *1776-1805* – Criticism and interpretation
  I. Title
  891.6'612   PB2297
  ISBN 0-7083-0954-2

Printed in England by J. W. Arrowsmith Ltd., Bristol

Preface

This study was originally commissioned by the Welsh Arts Council for the Writers of Wales series, and was published in a limited edition by the University of Wales Press in 1976, the bicentenary of Ann's birth. It went out of print in 1981. I am grateful to the Council and the Press for arranging the publication of this new edition, and in particular to Susan Jenkins for much help in preparing the text for the press.

The resetting of the text has enabled me to make some changes. I have rewritten the opening pages and made a number of alterations and additions, mainly intended to situate Ann more clearly in her own time and place. The substance of the book remains, however, unchanged. I have seen no reason to alter my original estimate of the greatness of this still little-known figure. With the present rapidly increasing interest in the study of spirituality it seems particularly important that the stature of Ann Griffiths should be more widely recognized. She holds a unique place in the spiritual history of our island.

I must again, as in the first edition, acknowledge my indebtedness to the late Professor H.A. Hodges, whose translations are used throughout this book. Without his help it could never have been written. Herbert Hodges died in the summer of 1976 at the very time it was first published. Working on it again I have constantly heard echoes of his voice.

Ash Wednesday 1986

A.M. Allchin

I

This book contains the story of a woman who lived from 1776, the year of American independence, to 1805, the year of the battle of Trafalgar. It was a brief life lived in a restricted space, most of it on a hill-farm in Montgomeryshire in mid Wales. It coincided with great events in the world outside, the revolution in France, the beginnings of the industrial revolution in Britain. But Ann Griffiths's life was not much touched by these things. She speaks to us of a different order of reality from theirs, of great but silent events in the world within us, of revolutions of another kind. Hers was a life lived at the point of intersection of the timeless with time, a life full of the many dimensions of eternity. It was a life centred on matters of ultimate concern, on questions of eternal significance, which can touch us today as they touched her then.

Ann Griffiths, as we shall seek to show, is a mystic and a theologian of uncommon power, one who saw deeply into the things of God and declared what she saw in memorable words. She is one whose name deserves to have a permanent place not only in the history of her own country, Wales, but of Britain as a whole. She can bear comparison with the greatest of our hymn-writers. Ann speaks of the mystery of Christ and the depths of God's love as things which we can know and enter into here and now. At times she knew God's grace as a consuming fire, at others as a cleansing, healing stream. 'Thanks always', she writes, 'that the furnace and the fountain are so close together.' She opens up dimensions of existence, human and divine, of which we are often almost wholly unaware.

Saunders Lewis, the greatest Welsh writer of this century, has spoken of the crisis of our time as a crisis of meaninglessness rather than of guilt. Faced with the horrors of Auschwitz and Buchenwald, with the threat of nuclear destruction, we ask whether life can have any meaning at all. To such a question Ann replies with her whole

1

being. Her whole life has become an act of worship. 'Ann is a poet', he writes, 'putting off her shoes from her feet, because the ground on which she stands at Llanfihangel-yng-Ngwynfa is holy ground. Where there is an object of worship, there cannot be a moment's doubt that life has an eternal meaning, that meaning is everywhere in the universe, and *Y greadigaeth ynddo'n symud* (all creation is moving in him).' So from this life, outwardly so narrow, from this work so apparently insignificant – all we have of hers are some thirty hymns and eight letters – something of incalculable value is given. We find here such a quality of vision, such an exploration of the heights and depths of human experience, such a statement of the central affirmations of the Christian faith, as to make of these things a precious element not only in the tradition of these islands but of the whole of humankind; a kind of focal point in which many things from far and near are gathered. Something has happened in the little house at Dolwar Fach in the parish of Llanfihangel-yng-Ngwynfa which makes of that place a spot memorable for more than one age and for more than one people.

II

Ann Griffiths was born in 1776 and died in August 1805 at the age of twenty-nine. Her father, John Evan Thomas, who had died in 1804 was a tenant farmer of some standing in his local community, who had more than once been church-warden. Her mother, Jane Thomas, died in 1794 when Ann was eighteen, and since both her elder sisters were already married, Ann from that time on became mistress of the household and remained so until her death. It was a hospitable household, not without its social life. In her early years Ann had the reputation of being a great one for parties and mad on dancing. As far as travelling is concerned we know that she frequently went to the nearest market town, Llanfyllin, about six miles distant to the east, and that after her conversion she went as often as possible on the monthly Communion Sundays to Bala, twenty-two miles over the Berwyn hills, to hear Thomas Charles preach and to receive the sacrament at his hands. As to further journeys we know nothing. Ann who uses the image of the sea with such effect, had probably never seen the sea.

The little house where she lived, Dolwar Fach, stands about two and a half miles south of Llanfihangel-yng-Ngwynfa and a little over one mile north of the hamlet of Dolanog, where there is now an Ann Griffiths Memorial Chapel. It is an isolated farmhouse, in a countryside of steep hills and swift streams, good land but not easy, lying between the barren uplands of the Berwyns to the north and the gentler valley pastures around places like Meifod and Llanfair Caereinion to the south. It was a working farm in the eighteenth century, and is still a working farm today. The family which lives there now is the same family which took over the tenancy in 1806, the year after Ann's death. They are much aware of the fact that their house is also a place of pilgrimage, and are wonderfully welcoming to those who come to visit it. In Ann's day this part of Montgomeryshire was well known for its ballads and folk-songs, its carols and interludes. Bala was a centre for local festivals of poetry and singing; a particularly notable *eisteddfod* of this kind took place in 1789, when Ann would have been thirteen. Composing verses for special occasions is a much commoner accomplishment in Welsh-speaking Wales than it is in England or Scotland. Ann's father had a certain skill in this. All this forms part of the background to Ann's life in the years before her conversion.

In her lifetime Ann was to be touched by the three major religious influences active at that time in rural Wales – first the Church, then the 'old Dissenters' with their roots in the seventeenth century, and finally the new movement of the Methodist revival. She grew up in the parish church at Llanfihangel-yng-Ngwynfa and became familiar there with the prayers and praises of the *Llyfr Gweddi Gyffredin*, the Welsh translation of the Book of Common Prayer. Although she went beyond this tradition after her conversion, that was the church in which she was married, and it is there that she lies buried. At a crucial moment in her life she was greatly influenced by the Independents (Congregationalists) and she remained in contact with their chapel at Llanfyllin till the end of her life. But it was with the Methodists that she found her home. Thomas Charles was the preacher she valued most, and John Hughes the friend to whom she confided her inmost hopes and fears. It is interesting that in our own century she has attracted the attention of Christians of every major denomination, not least Roman Catholic, who have seen in her many of the qualities to be found in their own contemplative saints.

We do not know exactly when the influence of Methodism first began to touch the family at Dolwar Fach. But by 1796 her elder brother John and her younger brother Edward were both deeply involved in the movement; Ann's own conversion probably dates from the following year. From that time onwards the family which had been deeply attached to the parish church became more and more identified with the Methodist cause. When after her father's death, Ann married, naturally enough she chose a leading local Methodist, Thomas Griffiths, a farmer of Meifod. So Nansi Thomas became Mrs Ann Griffiths, acquiring the name by which she has always since been known. Less than a year later she died, two weeks after the birth and death of her only child Elizabeth. She was buried in the churchyard at Llanfihangel on 12 August 1805.

4

Ann's life can only be understood against the background of the great evangelical movement of the eighteenth century, which in Wales took the form of Calvinistic Methodism. The movements in England and Wales were closely linked but in many ways independent of one another. Both however, took their origin towards the end of the first half of the eighteenth century.

In Wales during the first generation the main centres of the movement were in the south. The three outstanding figures were Daniel Rowland of Llangeitho (1713-90), William Williams, Pantycelyn (1717-91), and Howell Harris (1714-73) whose name is linked with the community of Trefeca. It was only during the second generation, roughly from 1780 to 1810, the period covering Ann's life, that its influence began to be strongly felt in the north. Here the outstanding personality was Thomas Charles of Bala, a man who had been ordained in the Church of England, but who now ministered in his own private chapel. Although the Methodists already formed a world of their own, the decisive split with the Church of England had not yet taken place in Wales at this time. This was to come in 1811, when for the first time the Welsh Methodists ordained their own ministers. Charles was a considerable preacher and a man of some learning. He was a man of more than local reputation, whose name is linked with the founding of the British and Foreign Bible Society. The large Bible Dictionary which he published in the year of Ann's death tells us much of how the Bible was studied and interpreted in the circles where he taught, and helps us to understand the way in which Ann interprets the Old Testament in the light of the New, constantly seeing the Person of Christ in the pages of the prophets and the psalms.

In England as in Wales, in all its different forms, Wesleyan as well as Calvinist, within the Church of England as well as outside it, the evangelical movement was one of an intense religious fervour. Its whole aim was to bring men and women to a saving knowledge of God. But as sometimes happens in Church history – we may think of the early years of Franciscanism – what begins as a revival of a purely religious nature soon gives rise to an interest in things of a more intellectual kind. It was so here. The part played by the Methodist revival in creating a large and serious minded body of readers in Welsh is familiar to all who care about the Welsh language. It is one of the major factors in the cultural history of Wales during

5

the last two centuries. People had to learn to read and write in order to be able to read the Scriptures, to come to a firsthand knowledge of the Word of God. They did so in their own language. Having done that they wanted to go further and to learn Greek and Hebrew in order to read the texts in the original. And they did this, too. Under the impulse of an awakening of faith and devotion an intellectual awakening took place, which caused farmers and housewives, shopkeepers and shepherds to ponder long and deeply on the ultimate issues of human life. All this is not irrelevant to a consideration of Ann. In her writings we shall find a remarkable fusion of intellect and feeling, of love and knowledge. No one could question the reality of the fervour; perhaps it is the intellectual power and clarity which strike us more.

Another of the characteristics of such a movement is that while it has a powerful personal and inward dimension, it grows out of intense shared experience. The power which this corporate enthusiasm can engender in its early stages, has a remarkable way of expanding men's vision and their capacity for action. Consider for a moment the little Methodist meeting, of which Ann was a member at Pontrobert. It contained three Johns, all of them men of character and initiative. There was first John Thomas, Ann's elder brother, the first of his family to be caught up into the movement, and the one who gradually brought the others into it after him. There was John Davies, a young man who having heard the call to be a missionary went with the London Missionary Society to Tahiti, and spent the rest of his life there. Finally there was John Hughes, a weaver's apprentice, who became first a teacher and eventually a minister. It was he who was Ann's closest friend and adviser in spiritual matters, who married her companion, Ruth Evans, and took down from her the words of Ann's hymns. If in Ann we find a quality of faith and vision which is in some way unique, we must remember that it arises out of the life and experience of a closely knit group of people of very different aptitudes. Aelred Squire, writing of the first generation of leaders of the Cistercian reform in the twelfth century, speaks of his impression of 'having encountered very individual personalities nurtured in a common climate of thought . . . In the presence of these writers one is haunted by a background of so many unknown eyes and faces. There is no way of recovering what all this meant, but it is certainly of more human importance than anything of which books can tell.' It is the same with the early Methodists; the preachers, the teachers, the hymn-writers give voice to the experience of a multitude of hidden men and women. We can gain from such a book as Morris Davies's *Cofiant Ann Griffiths*, published in 1856, some hint of what the shared assumptions and atmosphere of those early times were like. But constantly one is haunted by a background of so many unknown eyes and faces.

Ann's own part in the movement is clear. She gave expression to some of its deepest and most intimate longings, to some of its strongest and most firmly rooted convictions. But how did she find her way into it? The family in which she grew up was one which took its church membership seriously. Daily prayers taken from the Book of Common Prayer were the rule at Dolwar Fach. The family went to church on Sundays, and when they were unable to go, the dog went just the same. Education was not altogether neglected. Ann had two or three years of schooling with Mrs Owen y Sais at Dolanog. She learned to read and write, and acquired a little colloquial English, but not enough to read books in that language. The writing of the one letter which is preserved in her own hand is beautiful and regular and strangely mature. But it is noticeable that there is scarcely any sign of punctuation. The quiet respectable religion in which she grew up, like the very brief education which she received, had its limitations. In the end it proved to be insufficient. It could not give that personal assurance of salvation which the Methodist preaching offered. First John, then her second brother Edward, then Ann herself underwent the experience of conversion and identified themselves with the Methodist cause.

In Ann's case the change seems to have begun with a sermon which she heard at Llanfyllin in the summer of 1796. It was a sermon preached in the open air, and arranged by the old established Independent congregation at Capel Pen-dref. The preacher described a seriousness of Christian commitment which Ann did not know, and she was deeply troubled by his message. At Christmas she found herself going to the parish church alone, weeping and discouraged, since both her brothers were going to the Methodist meeting. She arrived very early before the commencement of the special early morning service, known as the *plygain*. Afterwards the vicar invited her in to breakfast. We do not know what exactly he then said, but we may gather that he made disparaging remarks about the new movement of religious enthusiasm. Whatever it was, it profoundly shocked and disgusted Ann. From this moment on there came a decisive break with the parish church, and shortly afterwards she found conversion.

Ann had always been a leader in the circles in which she lived, prominent alike for her high spirits and her abilities. In her earlier days she had not been averse to making fun of her Methodist neighbours. 'There go the pilgrims on their way to Mecca', she would say of them as they set off to go to Communion Sundays at Bala. Now that she had been converted she went on the monthly pilgrimage herself, though she did not cease to be a leader, nor did her high spirits desert her, even if they were expressed in different ways. She took a prominent part in all the doings of the Methodists – entertaining itinerant preachers and attending the meetings of the *seiat*. In her there was found all the fervour of a religious awakening with all the natural zest of a forceful and attractive personality. But there was something more. Although brief in utterance at a prayer meeting, there was a particular urgency in her petitions. Sometimes she was seen in silent tears as she sat at her spinning wheel, the Bible open on the little table beside her. And then it began to be known that she had composed hymn verses, and that there were moments of visitation.

Let us consider the visitations first. Ann was carried away not only into tears, but at times, into moods of overwhelming exultation. At times there seems to have been something like a trance. A number of these incidents have been recorded for us, and sometimes particular hymn verses have been associated with them. But it would certainly be over-simplifying matters to suppose that the hymns were simply 'given' in such moments of ecstatic experience. Some of them seem to be directly related to matters discussed at the meeting of the *seiat*. Others, we feel sure, must have been the result of long reflection. How exactly Ann herself would have thought about them is something of which we cannot be wholly certain. But at least we can guess something of it from the way in which they have come down to us.

III

The way in which her writings have come down to us is one of the most remarkable things about Ann. It is one of the things which tells us something of the world she lived in and what was taken for granted in it. Almost all that we have in her own hand is the text of the letter written to Elizabeth Evans, and now kept in the National Library at Aberystwyth. The other seven letters which remain, exist only in copies made by their recipient John Hughes. As to the hymns, they have come to us through oral tradition. Ann, it seems, never made a fair copy of them. We know that she sometimes jotted them down on odd scraps of paper, but none of these has been preserved. What we have, again in John Hughes's handwriting, are the words which Ruth, his wife, dictated to him after Ann's death. It was this same Ruth who had been Ann's companion at Dolwar Fach. Being a good singer she had provided the tunes for the words which Ann had composed. Since she herself was unable to write, we may safely trust the accuracy of her memory.

Here is a striking example of the persistence of oral tradition at the beginning of the nineteenth century, and we ought not to underrate its significance. A writer of our own time, J. C. Campbell, remarks on this subject, 'It is always extraordinarily difficult to convey the feeling and atmosphere of a community where oral tradition and the religious sense are still very much alive, to people who have only known the atmosphere of the modern ephemeral, rapidly changing world of industrial civilisation. On the one hand there is a community of independent personalities where memories of men and events are often amazingly long (in the Gaelic-speaking outer Hebrides they go back to Viking times a thousand years ago), and where there is an ever present sense of the reality and existence of the other world of spiritual and psychic experience; on the other there is a standardised world where people live in a mental jumble of newspaper headings and BBC news bulletins, forgetting yesterday's as they read and hear today's ... where memories are so short that men often do not know the names of their grandparents ...' This contrast is of help to us in approaching the society of which Ann was a part, and gives us a clue to understanding the context in which she composed and the way in which she thought of her verses.

The massive work of Williams Pantycelyn and his contemporaries had established the central place of hymns in the Methodist movement in Wales. But Pantycelyn was a man of formal education, well aware of the hymn writing of his English colleagues and predecessors, familiar alike with Wesley and Watts; a writer moreover of numerous other works both in verse and in prose. These works, theological, historical, and pastoral, make of Pantycelyn a central figure in both the intellectual and the spiritual history of the movement. Ann, however much she may have been influenced by him, can hardly have thought of herself as a hymn-writer of the same kind. Clearly she had no sense of what we should call literary proprietorship. The verses which she was given, were given she believed, not for herself alone, but for all the members of the community to which she belonged. She at once shared them with Ruth, and thus they passed into use in the meetings of their own and neighbouring *seiats*, knowledge of them spreading rather in the way that knowledge of folk-songs spreads, from singer to singer. It is interesting in this connection to note that Ann's lines frequently contain additional syllables, over and above those strictly necessary metrically. This characteristic which they have in common with many folk-songs, made their singing a problem when more regular hymn tunes came to be adopted later in the nineteenth century and caused many alterations to be made in the published versions of them.

It is not being suggested that Ann thought of her hymns simply as a kind of sacred folk-song. It is difficult to suppose that the writer of some of the greatest of her verses did not feel a literary pride in what she had composed, even if her predominant sentiment was one of gratitude for what she had received. There is a depth and order in her writing which speaks of much intellectual effort. As Gerald Brenan remarks in his study of St John of the Cross, 'there is a density and complexity of allusion in these poems that prove the absurdity of supposing that he was merely an 'inspired' poet who wrote his poems in ecstasies. A long period of preparation, both conscious and unconscious, preceded their composition, and if the ease and sureness with which they spring up show that many of them owe their birth to effortless moments, they were no doubt followed by careful correction and adjustments'.

As we shall see, though Ann's formal education was very slight, she had a mind of uncommon capacity. There is an old handwritten book in the National Library at Aberystwyth which evidently belonged to the household at Dolwar Fach and which contains copies of ballads and poems by local poets. On one page Ann has written a couple of Bible verses in English and then tried out a word or two in that unfamiliar language. One word is 'Incomprehensibilyty'. We should have known it was her, even if she had not signed her name on the page.

One clue to the background of Ann's hymns is to be found in the importance of the carol-singing in her district, a practice which persists to this day. The carols were particularly linked with the *plygain*, the early morning service held at Christmas, but they were also sung at other times. They carried down into the eighteenth century something of the popular faith and devotion of the pre-Reformation centuries. As is the way with such things they were remarkably conservative both in form and in sentiment. They were also one of the few elements in the traditional folk culture of which the new religious movement did not disapprove. So a minor Methodist poet of the 1830s, Dafydd Hughes (1792-1860), *Eos Iâl*, could produce carols of a type which might well date from the seventeenth century or before, and which make rich use of the Old Testament imagery which Ann employs in her hymns. Here are a few verses of a carol of his still sung today in the Tanat valley:

Ar gyfer heddiw'r bore, 'n Faban bach, 'n Faban bach,
Y ganwyd gwreiddyn Jese, 'n Faban bach;
Y Cadarn ddaeth o Bosra,
Y Deddfwr gynt ar Seina,
Yr Iawn gaed ar Galfaria, 'n Faban bach, 'n Faban bach,
Yn sugno bron Mareia, 'n Faban bach.

Caed bywiol ddwfr Eseciel, ar lin Mair, ar lin Mair,
A gwir Feseia Daniel, ar lin Mair;
Caed bachgen doeth Eseia,
'R addewid roed i Adda,
Yr Alffa a'r Omega, ar lin Mair, ar lin Mair,
Mewn côr ym Methlem Jiwda, ar lin Mair.

11

Diosgodd Crist ei goron, o'i wir fodd, o'i wir fodd,
Er mwyn coroni Seion, o'i wir fodd;
I blygu ei ben dihalog
O dan y goron ddreiniog,
I ddioddef dirmyg llidiog, o'i wir fodd, o'i wir fodd,
Er codi pen yr euog, o'i wir fodd.

Am hyn, bechadur, brysia, fel yr wyt, fel yr wyt,
I 'mofyn am y noddfa, fel yr wyt;
I ti'r agorwyd ffynnon
A ylch dy glwyfau duon
Fel eira gwyn yn Salmon, fel yr wyt, fel yr wyt;
Gan hynny tyrd yn brydlon, fel yr wyt.

(On this day's morn was born a little Child, a little Child,
The root of Jesse was born, a little Child,
The Mighty one of Bozra,
The Lawgiver on Mount Sinai,
The Atonement won on Calvary, a little child, a little child,
Sucking at Mary's breast, a little child.

The living waters of Ezekiel, on Mary's knee, on Mary's knee,
The Daniel's true Messiah, on Mary's knee,
The wise child of Isaiah,
The promise given to Adam,
The Alpha and Omega, on Mary's knee, on Mary's knee,
In a stall in Bethlehem Judah, on Mary's knee.

Christ put aside his crown, of his free will, of his free will,
That Zion might be crowned, of his free will,
To bow his undefiled head,
Beneath the thorny crown,
To suffer angry scorn, of his free will, of his free will,
To raise the guilty's head, of his free will.

Hasten to him sinner, therefore, as you are, as you are,
To seek in him a refuge, as you are,
For you a well is opened
To wash your wounds, and make you
As pure as snow on Salmon, as you are, as you are,
So come without delaying, as you are.)

When we think of the area where Ann grew up as remote, that may only reflect our own city-centred narrowness. As J. C. Campbell reminds us, such places are sometimes rich in an oral culture which conveys to the present values from the distant past, and brings the world of eternity close to every day.

But while we ought not to ignore the possible influence on Ann of elements of the popular religious culture of her day, we are on much surer ground when we come to two books which we know that she must have constantly used and read – the Bible and the Book of Common Prayer. It was these which formed her heart and mind, and between them there can have been no rivalry. It is the Bible which must have first place, with the Prayer Book providing one of the principal ways by which its teaching was assimilated. We who are used to a multitude of books and periodicals, let alone to the bombardment of our senses by radio and television, can hardly imagine what these books must have meant in an age when printed matter was hard to come by, and the divine authority and origin of the Scriptures unquestioned. For Ann, as for Christians through many ages, the Bible was a whole world, a world in which one finds one's own condition mirrored, a world in which God's word is constantly to be heard addressing us.

Moreover the way in which the Bible was interpreted, on principles which in their main outline go back to the first Christian centuries, enabled the perceptive reader to see a unity in all the different books, which escapes our more historically conditioned minds. As the seventh of the Thirty Nine Articles declares, a text with which Ann would certainly have been familiar: 'The Old Testament is not contrary to the New; for both in the Old and New Testament everlasting life is offered to mankind by Christ, who is the only Mediator between God and man, being both God and man.' So in her hymns, which are woven out of a tissue of biblical quotation and allusion, Old Testament types are constantly seen in reference to Christ. It is so, for instance, in one of the most familiar of them, perhaps the one which is most universally loved amongst Welsh speaking Christians, 'Wele'n sefyll rhwng y myrtwydd ...' The mysterious figure of the horseman in the prophet Zechariah who appears with good news for Sion, is at once, and without question, taken as a type of Christ.

The same process can be seen at work in the way in which Ann handles the stories of the Old Testament. For her they are not episodes out of a remote past. They speak to her directly of God's dealings with his people, that people to which she herself belongs, and they speak of his mercy and judgement of nations and individuals now no less than in the past. She reads with faith and she reads with imagination, and distant incidents come to life with an extraordinary vividness. She writes in one of her letters to John Hughes,

> I have found much pleasure in meditating on the Shunammite woman who set aside a room on the wall for the man of God to rest in when he passed by, placing in it a bed, a table, a stool and a candlestick. Perhaps that woman, in her longing for the prophet, often paced the room, and found a satisfaction in watching for the man.

The experience of the woman in Palestine almost three thousand years before, becomes her own experience as she longs for the coming of John Hughes, the one person with whom she can speak altogether freely of spiritual things.

This is not just a sentimental or historical identification with a figure in the past. Through the surface meaning of the Scriptures Ann always sees deeper levels of significance, just as in her own life, the everyday events of life on the farm became the ways by which she entered into contact with eternal realities. She takes it for granted that a sacred text has many levels of interpretation. So the experience of waiting, of feeling the absence of one whose presence is greatly desired is immediately referred by her to a greater and more universal experience; the situation of the believer when the sense of the Lord's presence is removed, when God makes himself known to us only as a painful absence. The longing for the coming of the man of God is a symbol for the longing for the advent of God himself. And in this predicament 'it comforts the heart of a believer, in the absence of the *visible* countenance of her Lord, that in some sense the furniture is still there'. The furniture, that is to say the words and promises of Scripture, the articles of Christian belief, the common structures of faith and life are still present, even when the Lord seems to have gone. For we notice here one of the primary characteristics of Ann's mind, its great precision. She speaks of the absence of the visible countenance of the Lord. She knows in her faith that he is not really absent, even when he seems most painfully to be so. So in a few lines, she tells us her experience, places it in a long historical perspective and sees that history itself as pointing to an eternal reality, to an eternal now in which the distance between Shunem and Berwyn suddenly become of little significance.

One of the things which would have helped Ann to see the Scriptures in this way, was the fact that since her childhood she had constantly been meeting the texts of the Bible in the context of prayer. For in the Christian tradition, it is believed that it is in prayer that eternity touches time, that we are 'with angels and archangels and all the company of heaven'. The daily prayers at home taken from the Book of Common Prayer, the regular prayer of the parish church, Sunday by Sunday, would have introduced her to this particular way of using the Bible. Long before her conversion, habits of thought and attention were being built up, which later blossomed into her awareness of an eternal now. The word 'Today' for instance, used in the phrase 'Today if you will hear his voice', which occurs in the psalm always said at the beginning of Matins, acquires a great wealth of meaning and association, in this way, linking the present moment with an eternal action. But not only in the use of the Bible in worship did the past come forcibly into the present. Still more in the Holy Communion past, present and future were for her united in the coming of the Lord.

It is a noteworthy fact that in eighteenth-century Methodism, in Wales no less than in England, the sacrament of the Eucharist had a vital place. While, in the parish churches of the land, the sacrament was administered infrequently and sometimes with no great reverence, amongst the Methodists there was a real revival of sacramental practice and devotion. At Llangeitho in the south for instance, where for years the preaching of Daniel Rowland attracted crowds from all over Wales, it was the Sacrament Sundays which often saw the largest congregations and the moments of greatest fervour. For the Methodists, both Welsh and English, the Communion was a 'converting ordinance'. On the monument to Howell Harris which is to be found in the parish church at Talgarth, we read, 'Near the Altar lie the remains of Howell Harris Esquire, born at Trevecka, January 23rd, 1713/14 O.S. Here where his body lies, he was convicted of sin, had his pardon sealed, and felt the power of Christ's precious blood, at the Holy Communion'. For people such as these there could be no doubt but that the Sacrament no less than the Word stood at the heart of Christian worship.

In Ann's own life, the monthly journey to Bala on Communion Sundays became a moment of particular significance. Quite a number of the stories which we have about her relate to the expeditions over the mountains, usually in company, occasionally alone. We have a picture of the young people hurrying down the narrow valley towards Bala on the Sunday morning from the inn at Llanwddyn where they had stopped to spend the night. We hear of the return journey in the evening with Ann going over again the points which had been treated in the sermon. One verse of a hymn in particular, is linked with a return journey when Ann was by herself, riding this time, lost in meditation on the things she had heard, the things she herself had shared in.

> O ddedwydd awr tragwyddol orffwys
> Oddiwrth fy llafur yn fy rhan
> Ynghanol môr o ryfeddodau
> Heb weled terfyn byth, na glan;
> Mynediad helaeth byth i bara,
> I fewn trigfannau tri'n un,
> Dŵr i'w nofio heb fynd trwyddo,
> Dyn yn Dduw, a Duw 'n ddyn.

(O blessed hour of eternal rest from my labour, in my lot, in the midst of a sea of wonders with never a sight of an end or a shore; abundant freedom of entrance, ever to continue, into the dwelling places of the three in one, water to swim in, not to be passed through, man as God and God as man.)

The sacrament of the Eucharist is understood not only as the moment when the Christian looks back to the Last Supper and the act of offering which it initiated. It has also always been seen as a moment of anticipation, a foretaste of the final rejoicing which shall be ours in the Kingdom of heaven. The Gospels themselves are full of stories of dinner parties and shared meals, and the theme of a great and royal banquet recurs frequently in the parables of Jesus. This is how Ann herself found it to be; she found in the worship she shared in that Sunday in Bala, a promise of a perfect sabbath rest, an entry into the very life of the Triune God.

As we have already suggested Ann sees all this in terms of the classical Christian tradition, and expresses what she sees in words of remarkable precision. In this single verse she has referred us to two of the basic articles of the Christian faith, the one in God as Trinity, the other in the union of God with man in Christ. Through the Incarnation, man is enabled to enter into and share in that sea of wonders, that ocean of joy and love and mutual self-giving, which the tradition has sought to affirm exists in God himself, by saying that he is at once three and one. And in this verse, which has sometimes been cited to show that Ann believed in a kind of absorption mysticism, in which man is simply dissolved into God, we find, when we look more carefully, that what she says is something different. In being called to enter into that eternal rejoicing, man does not cease to wonder, does not cease to praise, does not cease to grow in knowledge and in love. Separation is destroyed, but not at the expense of man's annihilation. There is abundant freedom of entrance into a life which knows no ending.

How is it that Ann manages in this way to wed depth of feeling to intellectual lucidity? It is not, after all, so easily done. Eccentric figures, intense and sometimes powerful, with their idiosyncratic visions and their individual theories, are not lacking in the history of Christianity, particularly in the history of Protestantism. There is nothing of this in her writing; rather we find a classical balance and sobriety. How is it, again with her sense of being drawn into the very life and being of God, that she does not simply lose herself in 'oceanic feeling', or like Emily Brontë, only a few years later, find herself inventing a private language to express her experience? Where does this element of order and structure come from?

We have already hinted at one of its principal sources in speaking of the Book of Common Prayer. There Ann would have found in texts with which she had long been familiar, the Te Deum, and the Apostles' and the Nicene Creed, for instance, the outlines of that faith which she expounded. In the Athanasian Creed we may suppose that her enquiring mind would have found a particular fascination. What is certain is that her grasp of both Trinitarian and Christological doctrine is remarkably sound, as we see for instance in the verse of the hymn where she speaks of

> Dwy natur mewn un person
> Yn anwahanol mwy
> Mewn purdeb heb gymysgu
> Yn berffaith hollol trwy.

(Two natures in one person, inseparable henceforth, in purity without confusion, perfect through and through.)

Equally remarkable is her capacity to sum up in a few lines, a whole history of Christian teaching and experience. Speaking again of the person of Christ, in the following verse, she says

> Y mae'n ddyn i gydymdeimlo
> A'th holl wendidau i gyd,
> Mae'n Dduw i gario'r orsedd
> Ar ddiafol, cnawd, a byd.

(He is man to sympathise with all thy weaknesses together, he is God to win the throne over the devil, the flesh, and the world.)

When we come to ask in detail how much she might have read, it is very difficult to give a definite answer. Certainly not much in terms of modern reading habits, but perhaps more than we should at first expect. There was quite an amount of theological and spiritual writing available in Welsh in the later eighteenth century. It is more than possible that she could have read, for instance, a translation of Richard Baxter's book *The Saints' Everlasting Rest*. With its fervent meditations on the glory of heaven there is much in it which would have caught her attention. Again she might have known Bishop William Beveridge's *Particular Thoughts upon Religion*, a work which contains a remarkably clear exposition of the doctrine of the Trinity. In meeting such writers as these she would have been coming into contact with major figures in seventeenth-century Anglican and Puritan divinity, and it may be that it was through them that she got something of her own feeling for the shape and quality of Christian doctrine.

Standing behind such writers as these, there were of course the great Christian thinkers of the earliest centuries, whose names we may suppose she hardly knew, who had hammered out in the course of violent controversy the basic outline of the faith which she received through the Creeds and the liturgical formularies. Nearer to her own time, there was another towering figure of a comparable importance, John Calvin. The clarity of his grasp upon the essentials of the Christian faith, the particular emphasis which he laid on belief in the absolute sovereignty and majesty of God and his purposes for man from all eternity, are things which had come down to her through the whole weight of the teaching of the movement of which she was a part. Like John Hughes, with whom she doubtless discussed these matters and from whom certainly she learned much, she was altogether ready to receive the great positive affirmations of this most lucid of the sixteenth-century reformers. If, as we shall suggest, there are in Ann unexpected themes and emphases which remind us of older traditions of Christian theology than that of Calvin's Geneva, this does not mean that she was not deeply indebted to the stream of teaching which came from him.

This element of almost Gallic clarity in Ann's writing, both in her hymns and her letters, is perhaps one of the things which gives us a clue to understanding her position within the literary tradition of Wales. Ann belongs to that one Celtic nation which in the origins of its language and its literature was deeply touched by the order and discipline of the Roman Empire. In a great variety of ways that Latin influence has continued to be active in the cultural tradition of Wales. We may perhaps see in Ann's combination of intensity of feeling with clarity of thought, something of that fusion of different elements, which has played so great a part in shaping the inheritance of Wales. In her, the experience of the first age of the saints seems to live again. She presents us, in a time not so remote from our own, with a possibility of communion with what is most central and essential in the whole Christian tradition. In other Welsh writers of our own century no less than of hers, we feel a closeness to our origins, and a living contact with those sources of life which too easily are forgotten or obscured today.

IV

But let us move from the discussion of Ann's sources to a consideration of her hymns, and among them turn first to one of the best known of them. It is incidentally the only one to have found its way into the hymn-books in something like the form in which it was first written down, since in the case of almost all the others, verses have been re-arranged and amended to suit the taste of generations of editors. Even here the more correct word *llywydd* has been substituted for Ann's anglicism *peilat* in the second verse.

> Wele'n sefyll rhwng y myrtwydd
> Wrthrych teilwng o fy mryd,
> Er mai o ran yr wy'n adnabod
> Ei fod uwchlaw gwrthrychau'r byd;
> Henffych fore,
> Y caf ei weled fel y mae.
>
> Rhosyn Saron yw ei enw,
> Gwyn a gwridog, teg o bryd,
> Ar ddeng mil y mae'n rhagori,
> O wrthrychau penna'r byd;
> Ffrind pechadur,
> Dyma ei beilat ar y môr.
>
> Beth sy imi mwy a wnelwyf
> Ag eilunod gwael y llawr
> Tystio'r wyf nad yw eu cwmni
> Yw cystadlu â Iesu mawr;
> O am aros,
> Yn ei gariad ddyddiau f'oes.

(Behold standing among the myrtles an object worthy of my whole mind, although I know in part that he is above all objects in the world; hail to the morning when I shall see him as he is.

Rose of Sharon is his name, white and ruddy, fair of form, he is excellent above ten thousand of the chiefest objects in the world; Friend of the sinner, here is his pilot on the sea.

What have I to do any more with the base idols of earth? I testify that their company is not to be set in competition with the great Jesus; O to abide in his love all the days of my life.)

We have already remarked on the way in which the hymn begins with the figure of one of the angelic messengers of the Old Testament, and at once identifies him with the Christ, who is at once the Messenger and the Message from God. The first verse contains at least two further allusions to the Bible, this time to passages in the New Testament. Ann is full of wonder to see amidst the objects of this world one who is above all these objects, one who can command the assent of man's whole heart and mind in a way that no created thing can do. Here is all the paradox of the notion of incarnation. God the creator enters into his creation. Her knowledge of him now, she says, must be in part, thus echoing the words of St Paul at the end of one of the most famous passages in his letters, 'now I know in part, then I shall know even as I am known'. Like St Paul, this thought leads Ann forward to long for the time when 'that which is perfect is come and that which is in part shall be done away'. (1 Cor. 13, 12). 'Hail to the morning when I shall see him as he is.'

In this last line, however, there is also a reminiscence of the first Epistle of St John. 'Beloved now are we the sons of God, and it doth not yet appear what we shall be; but we know that when he shall appear we shall be like him, for we shall see him as he is.' (I John 3, 2). This passage, which like the words which have just been quoted from St Paul, has had an incalculable influence on the development of Christian experience through the ages, shows us again the tension between what is given now and what shall be given hereafter, beyond this world of space and time. This eager expectation, this movement towards the future, is something which Ann knows well. With her, as with all the great contemplatives down the ages, the vision of eternity, granted within the world of time, sets up an intense longing for its fulfilment in a realm beyond this one.

William of St Thierry in the twelfth century, having spoken eloquently of the moment of vision, puts it like this, 'For nowhere doth the mode of human imperfection become more manifest to itself than in the light of the countenance of God and the glass of divine vision;

where in the Day that is, seeing more and more what it lacketh, it amendeth daily by likeness that wherein it faileth by unlikeness; . . . For it is impossible that the Sovereign Good should be seen and not loved; or not loved as much as it hath been suffered to be seen; till love advance to some likeness of that love which did make God like to man in the humility of human estate, to the end that He might make man like to God in the glory of the partaking of the divine'. Here too there are echoes of the passage from St John just noted, which continues, 'And every man that hath this hope in him, purifieth himself, even as he is pure'.

This longing to be pure and faithful to the vision, is one which Ann expresses in the two subsequent verses of the hymn, and which we shall find again when we come to look at the contents of her letters. And in these verses, after the almost austere statement of the first line (an *object* worthy of my whole *mind*), we come to the more affective language of the Song of Songs, to the vision of the Lord as friend and guide through the perplexities of this life. Mind and heart together are caught up into the vision.

The final verse confronts us sharply with the question of Ann's attitude towards the created world. Are all the things which God has made, to be considered simply as idols, things to be rejected? There is no doubt that at times in Christian tradition the movement of turning away from the world to God has been made in a one-sided and exaggerated way. That this was sometimes the case in Wales in the nineteenth century is suggested by the emphasis with which many of the most deeply Christian poets of our own time have stressed the other side of the picture; that God is to be loved in and through all his works, and not apart from or against them. Evidently they have felt the need to reply to what seemed an unduly negative strain in the religion of the last century.

> Duw ni waharddodd inni garu'r byd,
> A charu dyn a'i holl weithredoedd ef . . .

(God has not forbidden us to love the world, and to love man and all his works . . .)

declares Gwenallt in the opening flourish of one of his finest sonnets. And more gently, but not less incisively, Euros Bowen takes this very line of Ann, 'What more have I to do?' and replies to it with the lines

Ond cymharu
Harddwch
A hyfrydwch
A mawredd
Â'r gerdd
Sydd yn eilunod gwael y llawr.

(But to compare beauty and delight and majesty with the poetry which is in the poor idols of the world.)

The point both poets are making is incontrovertible within any whole and balanced Christian view of the world. God is to be loved in all things, as well as above all things. To say anything else would imply a denial of the goodness of what he has made. But in reply to this criticism, which applies of course not only to Ann, but to the whole of the movement of which she was a part, two things need to be said. First, it is clear that Ann's position is not a wholly negative one. She finds all created things of little value, not because she despises them in themselves, but because she has seen something else, a vision of an eternal splendour with which they cannot compare. We may not share her experience, but we can hardly doubt its reality for her, or fail to acknowledge that many bear witness to it through the centuries. When compared with the greatness of God the creator, things of this world suddenly seem trivial; the whole creation is seen as very small, small as a hazel-nut held in the palm of the hand, as Julian of Norwich puts it in the fourteenth century. Ann says the same thing in different words,

Ni ddichon byd a'i holl deganau
    Foddloni fy serchiadau'n awr
A enillwyd, a ehangwyd
    Yn nydd nerth fy Iesu mawr;
Ef, nid llai, a eill eu llenwi,
    Er mor ddiamgyffred yw,
O am syllu ar ei berson,
    Fel y mae fe'n ddyn a Duw.

(The world and all its trinkets cannot now satisfy my affections, which have been captured, which have been widened in the day of the power of my great Jesus; he, and nothing less, can fill them, incomprehensible though he is – O to gaze upon his person, man and God as he is.)

But from the Christian point of view there is a second point to be made. To love God above and beyond all the things that he has made need not lead us to despise those things in themselves. Rather, as with Julian of Norwich, it may lead us to regard them as precious and good, despite their limitations and fragility. The movement away from the world to God may be followed by a movement back towards the world, seen now as the object of God's love. There is a dialectical movement here which in the end is essential to the maintenance of the Christian vision of the world as God's word and gift to us. Both sides are necessary. Only if we can see God's glory shining out beyond all things, shall we be able to see that same glory shining out in all things.

How far Ann herself would have been able to make that second step it is impossible to say. There were strands in the teaching of Welsh Methodism – its comparative neglect of the doctrine of creation for instance, and its great stress on the sinfulness and corruption of man – which would have made it difficult. Ann's unexpected emphasis on the doctrine of man's creation in God's image and likeness suggests that she was not altogether unaware of these problems. It is possible too to regard her decision to marry as an expression of a more mature and balanced hold upon the twin ways of affirmation and rejection. What does seem clear is that in practice, if not in theory, a grasp upon the potentially sacramental nature of the world seems to have been present in many parts of Welsh Nonconformity throughout the nineteenth century. Whether, because life was lived in such close contact with the natural order, or because of an unconscious hold upon earlier traditions, Christian and even pre-Christian, the negative and censorious face of the movement was not by any means always predominant. The society described by D. J. Williams in the first volume of his autobiography, *The Old Farmhouse*, is not a notably life-denying nor outwardly religious one. But when he tells us of his father that 'His great gift was the gift of prayer. It was a joy to listen to him when he knelt', we are made to pause. Still more, when speaking of his mother he confides 'She was quite selfless and without any desire to be seen. Her treasure was her inward life ... She did not speak much of her religion beyond praising the goodness she saw in others and being tender towards their weaknesses ... It is my belief that her life, every minute of it as it came, was all one secret prayer', we recognize at once the world of which Ann's letters speak. Something of the experience of the first Methodist generations lived on in the chapel at Rhydcymerau, as in many other places, at the beginning of our own century and contributed to a life in which grace and nature were at one.

As regards Ann there is much that we cannot know. What we have in her letters and her hymns is the testimony of one who, in her mid-twenties, has looked deeply into the things of eternity and been so dazzled by the splendour of what she has seen that she has no eyes for anything else. Her mind and her affections have alike been captured and enlarged. Nowhere is this combination of intellectual and affective insight more in evidence than in the greatest of her hymns, so striking at once in its content and in its fervour. As Saunders Lewis says, it is rightly to be regarded as 'one of the majestic songs in the religious poetry of Europe'.

> Rhyfedd, rhyfedd gan angylion,
>   Rhyfeddod fawr yng ngolwg ffydd,
> Gweld rhoddwr bod, cynhaliwr helaeth
>   A rheolwr pob peth sydd,
> Yn y preseb mewn cadach[au]
>   Ac heb le i roi ben i lawr,
> Ac eto disglair lu'r gogoniant
>   Yn ei addoli ef yn awr.
>
> Pan bo Seinai i gyd yn mygu,
>   A swn yr utgorn uwcha'i radd
> Caf fynd i wledda tros y terfyn
>   Yng Nghrist y Gair heb gael fy lladd;
> Mae yno'n trigo bob cyflawnder,
>   Llond gwagle colledigaeth dyn;
> Ar y adwy rhwng y ddwyblaid
>   Gwnaeth gymod trwy ei offrymu ei hun.

(Wonderful, wonderful in the sight of angels, a great wonder in the eyes of faith, to see the giver of being, the generous sustainer and ruler of everything that is, in the manger in swaddling clothes and with nowhere to lay his head, and yet the bright host of glory worshipping him now.

When Sinai is altogether on smoke, and the sound of the trumpet at its loudest, in Christ the Word I can go to feast across the boundary without being slain; in him all fullness dwells, enough to fill the gulf of man's perdition; in the breach, between the parties, he made reconciliation through his self-offering.)

The first verse begins with an exclamation of wonder, of amazement before the mystery of the incarnation. It is very striking and very typical of Ann that she should begin at this point. The whole emphasis of the Evangelical movement of which Methodism was a part, was on the problem of man's sin, his guilt before the righteousness of God. Hence the cardinal point in all its preaching was the doctrine of the atonement, the explanation of the way in which God's forgiveness comes to man through the sacrificial death of Christ upon the Cross. All this, as we shall see, is central also for Ann. But she places this problem within the context of a wider, deeper mystery about God's relationship with man, one which the Evangelicals never denied, but tended to pass over somewhat rapidly. For her the basic problem is that of man's finitude and God's infinity, and so for her the starting point is the belief that he who is 'the giver of being, the generous sustainer and ruler of everything that is', has entered into his creation and accepted the limitations of our human state, vividly symbolized by the swaddling clothes in which the infant Jesus is wrapped. Thus the doctrine of man's redemption is placed within the doctrine of God's incarnation, God's coming in flesh to be where man is, so that by his gift man may be raised up to where he is.

This thought of man's ascent to God follows on directly in the second verse of the hymn. How can man go up to God? Here we have one of the most remarkable examples of the way in which Ann restates a basic theme of Christian spirituality which she can hardly have known directly through her reading. The story of Moses going up to speak with God in the cloud on Mount Sinai, was taken by the theologians of the early centuries, Gregory of Nyssa for example, as an image of the way in which the believing heart and mind must approach the presence of the inaccessible God. Only as he goes up through the cloud and the darkness, setting aside his own ideas and concepts, his own images and desires, can man become apt to receive the revelation which God wills to give us of himself. No man can see God and live. There is a death to self which is inescapable on this way. But in Christ the Word, in whom man and God are fully reconciled and at one, this death no longer has terror. Our death is

included in his death, our life is united with his triumphant life. In
him the barriers erected by sin and guilt, the barriers of death itself
are taken away.

So we come to the two central verses of the hymn.

> Efe yw'r Iawn fu rhwng y lladron,
> Efe ddioddef angau loes,
> Efe a nerthodd freichiau ei ddienyddwyr
> I'w hoelio yno ar y groes;
> Wrth dalu dyled pentewynion
> Ac anrhydeddu deddf ei Dad,
> Cyfiawnder, mae'n disgleirio'n danbaid
> Wrth faddau yn nhrefn y cymod rhad.
>
> O f'enaid, gwel y man gorweddodd
> Pen brenhinoedd, awdwr hedd,
> Y greadigaeth ynddo'n symud,
> Yntau'n farw yn y bedd;
> Cân a bywyd colledigion,
> Rhyfeddod fwya angylion nef,
> Gweld Duw mewn cnawd a'i gydaddoli
> Mae'r côr dan weiddi 'Iddo Ef'.

(He is the Satisfaction that was between the thieves, he suffers the
pains of death, it was he who gave to the arms of his executioners the
power to nail him there to the cross; when he pays the debt of brands
plucked out of the burning, and honours his Father's law, Righteousness shines with fiery blaze as it pardons within the terms of the free
reconciliation.

O my soul, behold the place where lay the chief of kings, the author
of peace, all creation moving in him, and he lying dead in the tomb;
song and life of the lost, greatest wonder of the angels of heaven, the
choir of them sees God in flesh and worships him together, crying out
'Unto him'.)

He 'is the satisfaction which was between the thieves'. The word
'iawn' (satisfaction) has a multitude of meanings in Welsh. It means
what is right, what is fitting, what is true. In the midst of man's
failure, his thieving, his wasting of God's gift, God himself comes to
be in man the reconciliation; to be in that place the new source of
goodness, the new source of truth. The paradoxes which are so
characteristic of Ann's style are heightened to an ever increasing
degree, and we cannot but think of the verses in the Byzantine

rite for Good Friday, of which, of course, she could have had no knowledge.

> He who clothes himself with light as with a garment,
> Stands naked at the judgement.
> On his cheek he received blows
> From the hands which he had formed.

Or again

> Today is hanged upon the tree
> He who hanged the earth in the midst of the waters.
> A crown of thorns crowns him
> Who is the King of the angels.
> He is wrapped about with the purple of mockery
> Who wraps the heaven in clouds.

The verse which expounds the mystery of the Cross, leads us on to the lines which expound the mystery of the tomb, of Christ's descent among the dead. Here Ann gives us what is without any question her most startling image, which sees the creator and redeemer of all, lying dead in the tomb, 'all creation moving in him'. Some of the greatest Christian thinkers of our own time, Hans Urs von Balthasar for instance, have underlined the relevance of this particular article of faith for our own age. Christ's descent into the place of death, the place of separation from God, is an element of the Christian tradition which can speak most powerfully to a civilization which has a fearful sense of alienation from the roots of being and of meaning. By taking man's alienation, man's death into himself, God raises up all men into new possibilities of life. In this respect the Eastern Orthodox icon of the resurrection is extremely eloquent. This shows Christ, not as a solitary figure rising from the grave, but rather as the victor over death drawing up with him Adam and Eve (in their role as the representatives of all mankind). However, Ann's image of the prince of life lying dead in the tomb, the forces of life still latently present within him, is an infinitely suggestive one, gathering together elements from the mythology and poetry of many ages and many people. The sleeping Lord will one day return. But here his awakening has already taken place; life shines forth from the tomb. He who descended is already ascended. Man's flesh which has been imprisoned is already set free, and before God all the heavenly powers rejoice. Again in the

28

juxtaposition of death and resurrection, and in the association of human with angelic praises there are remarkable parallels with the Byzantine hymnody for Holy Week,

> I magnify thy sufferings,
> I praise thy burial and thy resurrection
> Proclaiming, Lord, glory to thee.

What is being said here is that the substance of human existence, personal and historical (man's flesh, the stuff of his life) is not doomed to futility and death but is lifted up into the infinite possibilities of the eternity of God. Man's fear of death, his fear of meaninglessness is overcome. There is an object of worship, God in flesh; and not mankind alone but all creation can enter into union with him.

So the hymn which up till this moment has been centred upon the mystery of that object, tracing his journey from Bethlehem to the Cross, from the empty tomb to the mount of ascension, now takes on a more purely personal, even subjective tone.

> Diolch byth, a chanmil diolch,
> Diolch tra bo yno'i chwyth
> Am fod gwrthrych i'w addoli
> A thestun cân i bara byth;
> Yn fy natur, wedi ei demtio
> Fel y gwaela' o ddynol ryw,
> Yn ddyn bach, yn wan, yn ddinerth,
> Yn anfeidrol wir a bywiol Dduw.

> Yn lle cario corff o lygredd,
> Cyd-dreiddio â'r côr yn danllyd fry
> I ddiderfyn ryfeddodau
> Iechydwriaeth Calfari,
> Byw i weld yr Anweledig
> Fu farw ac sy'n awr yn fyw,
> Tragwyddol anwahanol undeb
> A chymundeb â fy Nuw.

> Yno caf ddyrchafu'r Enw
> A osododd Duw yn Iawn
> Heb ddychymyg llen na gorchudd,
> A'm henaid ar ei ddelw'n llawn;

Yng nghymdeithas y dirgelwch
Datguddiedig yn ei glwy
Cusanu'r mab i dragwyddoldeb
Heb im' gefnu arno mwy.

(Thanks for ever, and a hundred thousand thanks, thanks while there is breath in me, that there is an object to worship and a theme for a song to last for ever; in my nature, tempted like the lowest of mankind, a babe, weak, powerless, the infinite true and living God.

Instead of carrying a body of corruption, to penetrate ardently with the choir above into the endless wonders of the salvation wrought on Calvary, to live to see the Invisible who was dead and now is alive – eternal inseparable union and communion with my God!

There I shall exalt the Name which God has set forth to be a Propitiation, without imagination, curtain or covering and with my soul fully in his likeness; in the fellowship of the mystery revealed in his wounds, I shall kiss the son to all eternity, and never turn from him any more.)

'Thanks for ever, and a hundred thousand thanks, thanks while there is breath in me . . .' Man's power to praise, man's capacity to rejoice is made free. With all the powers of heaven he can glorify God and give thanks for the wonder of the Word made flesh. There is a tone of ecstasy in verses five and six. Again the play of paradox is an essential element in the writer's strategy, taking us beyond our customary use of concepts and images, forcing us to re-interpret them, to let them be transfigured and transformed. But as we should expect with Ann the movement beyond, the movement of ecstasy is lucid and sober. The precision remains. The union of the believer with God is eternal and inseparable, but it involves no confusion or mingling. It is a communion without intermediary, made possible by the full restoration of the image of God in man, that capacity for God which is latent in every man. It is a union which, at the supreme moment of her song, Ann can only express in terms of the kiss exchanged between the belover and the beloved, the bridegroom and the bride.

And here surely we must pause for a moment. In many ways one would prefer to let these lines in all their simplicity speak for themselves, and to remain silent before them. But with their close juxtaposition of love and suffering depicted under such vivid imagery they could be taken perhaps to suggest some unhealthy eroticism.

There are curious by-paths in the history of Christian devotion. What here is the mystery of the wounds doing so close to the embrace of the beloved?

In a preliminary way we must notice two things. First, Ann is very reticent on the subject of the sufferings of Christ. The absolute centrality of his sacrificial death within the scheme of salvation is never in question in any of her writings. But a detailed and painful meditation on the incidents of the passion, something which had been common enough in the devotional writing of Catholicism and Protestantism alike, is wholly absent from her. It is the simple thought of 'who it is that was on the cross' which arrests her mind in amazement. That the generosity and love of eternity should be present in, and in some way active through the most sordid, in-explicable elements of man's experience, this is what captures her attention as it has done that of Christians throughout the ages. It is this which she points to in speaking of the mystery revealed in the wounds.

Secondly, in reference to the kiss of the last line of all, we must notice that though the words of the Song of Songs seem constantly to be at the back of her mind, she is very sparing in explicit use of the imagery of bride and bridegroom to describe the relationship of the soul with God. In one of her letters she speaks of her longing for a 'marriage union' with God in his Son. In one of her hymns she speaks of the Cross as her husband's Cross. But that is all. This also is a place where Christian devotion has at times run into strange extravagances. We do not find them in Ann.

And here a second point has to be understood. Both images, the fellowship of the wounds, and the kiss of the beloved, carry with them a weight of hidden significance. Both phrases have scriptural overtones which give them a whole range of further associations. The words 'Kiss the Son' for instance occur in Psalm 2, v. 12 ('Kiss the son, lest he be angry, and so ye perish from the way') and are quoted by Ann in a quite different context. That the words as they occur in the hymn are full of personal longing we need not deny. But they are something more than an expression of purely personal feeling. They form part of a sacred traditional text, which gives to them a certain objectivity and perspective, so that what is deeply personal does not become merely subjective, let alone sentimental. 'To kiss the Son', not lest he be angry, but so as never to turn from him any more, that is her desire, the desire which elsewhere she expresses in terms of her longing to be steadfast, to abide; to know the assurance of eternity and never to depart from it again.

Perhaps a parallel taken from a great Christian poem of our own century may help us to appreciate what Ann is saying here. *In Parenthesis* by David Jones is a very different kind of work from the hymns which we are considering. But it too contains much about wounds and death, because so much of it is about the experience of the ordinary foot-soldier in the trenches in Flanders in the First World War. It could be a profoundly depressing book, yet it is not. Throughout it there is a suggestion, implicit rather than explicit, that in and through the suffering and the sordidness, something of goodness is being revealed. As the author says in the preface, 'We find ourselves privates in foot regiments. We search how we may see formal goodness in a life singularly inimical, hateful to us'. This suggestion that somehow what is evil is being redeemed by love becomes explicit only on the very last page of the book. There we are given six quotations from the Bible, three in the Latin of the Vulgate, three in the English of the Authorised Version. Thus it is made clear that while this is a very personal statement it is also a traditional one, gathering up the experience and the wisdom of many ages. Again it is done so as to distance us a little from the unbelievable poignancy of what is being said. For these quotations speak to us of the scapegoat which carries away the people's sins, of the lamb slain as a sacrificial victim, of the author of all form and comeliness without any form or comeliness; they speak to us of the suffering of Christ in the suffering of his people, and they conclude with the words from the Song of Songs, 'This is my beloved, and this is my friend'.

Yes, suffering and love are closely intermingled in human experience, and sometimes in perverse and destructive ways. The Christian tradition, when it is true to itself, is not afraid to enter into the dark and instinctual places of the human heart and mind; it would not have had very much power if it had not been willing to do so. But always it has believed that through the mystery of Christ the whole of man is bought back and redeemed; that in him suffering itself becomes the way by which creative love is made free; and that that creative and forgiving love is able to bring man to the eternal fulfilment for which in the beginning he was made.

V

We have constantly to remember that the life which is reflected in the hymns was being lived in the day-to-day routine of a small farm in the Berwyns. There was a great deal to be done around the house and in the stockyard, and it would not always have been easy to reconcile the demands of the vision of ultimate and eternal realities with the requirements of every day.

We see something of the tension involved in Ann's letters. In one she writes,

> I am sometimes absorbed so far into these things that I completely fail to stand in the way of my duty with regard to temporal things . . .

From the stories which have come down to us we can guess at some of the incidents she is referring to. Ann would be found in the kitchen, apparently unware of all around her. A hymn was on the way. She would go out to the potato shed, but then not come back. After a time they would go and look for her and find her wholly lost in thought.

But there is much more to it than that. Reading Ann's letters we get the impression that there were periods of intense inner conflict. In the very first one she writes to John Hughes,

> I should be glad to speak of my own experience. I have had some rather smart trials and strong winds, so that I was almost out of breath on the slopes . . .

And then, quoting two texts of Scripture which have helped her, she adds

> I thought to pull myself up the hill by the two following chains . . . It was quiet and warm for a while.

This vivid way of speaking of inner trials in terms of daily experience on the hills continues in later letters. But the sense of conflict grows stronger,

> I have been finding it very stormy for a long time. I have had very many disappointments in myself without a break ... I have lately been particularly far gone in spiritual whoredom from the Lord ...

or again,

> The warfare is as hot as it ever was, enemies within, enemies without.

What are we to make of such avowals?

First of all it is clear that Ann is living by very exalted standards. She seeks to abide in a vision of eternity, while living in the midst of the changes of time. The overwhelming sense which she had of seeing into eternal things made demands on her whole life which it is difficult for us fully to enter into. 'Of all things' she writes, 'it is the sin of thought which presses most heavily on me ...' In another letter she explains this more fully.

> The most pressing thing that is on my mind is the sinfulness of any visible thing obtaining a leading place in my mind. I am full of shame and reverence, and I rejoice in astonishment to think that he for whom it is a condescension to look upon the things of heaven has also given himself as an object of love to a creature as vile as I.

Here is the clue to understanding the sins and trials of which Ann speaks, her constant disappointment with herself. These things spring from her acute sense that if God can occupy the first place in man's heart and man's mind, then it is a betrayal of his love, a denial of the very source of life and meaning, to allow anything else to take that first place. It is an infidelity, a refusal of his infinite generosity. Seen in this context, the language about spiritual harlotry, which of course is biblical in origin, does not seem so exaggerated. Clearly Ann allows that other things must enter in, must have their rightful place in man's heart and mind, but even the best created things must never come before God. Taken in comparison with him, who is by definition beyond all comparison, what are they but idols? And if this is the case with what is good, what about the hundred and one frivolous, trivial, unimportant thoughts and desires which flit through the mind in the course of a day? What about the malicious and destructive ones? It is in this perspective that we may hope to understand her 'longing to be pure', and her prayer to be steadfast and faithful to the vision. We remember that it is promised to the pure in heart that they shall see God, and we remember too, Kierkegaard's word, 'Purity of heart is to will one thing'.

As she went on along this perplexing path she grew in maturity. The letters cover a period of at most four years, and the dating of some of them is not altogether clear. But we can feel between the first and the last a definite growth in self-knowledge. She became more accustomed to the paradoxes involved in trying to live at different levels simultaneously, and discovered that alternations of light and darkness, times of stress and times of quiet, were an integral part of the way. Patience was needed, she found, as well as urgency. We must constantly be moving forward, but always be able to stand still and know by anticipation that completion which will be granted only in its fullness in the end of all things. She expresses this with a wonderful triple paradox in one hymn verse,

> Mi gerdda'n ara' ddyddiau f'oes
> Dan gysgod haeddiant gwaed y groes;
>   A'r yrfa redaf yr un wedd;
> Ac wrth ei rhedeg sefyll wnaf –
> Gweld iachawdwriaeth lawn a gaf
>   Wrth fynd i orffwys yn y bedd.

(I shall walk slowly all the days of my life, under the shadow of the merit of the blood of the cross, and I shall run the course in the same way, and as I run I shall stand still and see the full salvation that I shall find when I come to rest in the grave.)

As she followed this way, however, she found that there were other possibilities of sinning against the light; not only that she might allow secondary things to come first in her thoughts and affections, but that she might allow her own ideas, her own imaginings to take the place of the mysteries which God was revealing to her. To understand her anxieties here we have to remember how seriously she would have taken the idea that the articles of Christian faith are not man's invention but God's own disclosure of himself, so that to fail to receive them lucidly and in due proportion is to dishonour him, and to risk cutting oneself off from the very source of

35

truth and light. If we wish to see how deeply she thought about this matter, to what a remarkable degree pure theology was important for her, we need to consider the following passage from the letter to Elizabeth Evans.

> Dear sister, the most outstanding thing that is on my mind at present as a matter for thought is to do with grieving the Holy Spirit. That word came into my mind, "Know ye not that your bodies are temples of the Holy Spirit which dwelleth in you"; and on penetrating a little into the wonders of the Person, and how he dwells or resides in the believer, I think in short that I have never been possessed to the same degree by reverential fears of grieving him, and along with that I have been able to see one reason, and the chief reason, why this great sin has made such a slight impression upon my mind, on account of my base and blasphemous thoughts about a Person so great.
>
> This is how my thoughts ran about the Persons of the Trinity. I feel my mind being seized by shame, and yet under a constraint to speak because of the harmfulness of it. I thought of the persons of the Father and the Son as co-equal; but as for the Person of the Holy Spirit, I regarded him as a functionary subordinate to them. O what a misguided imagination about a Person who is divine, all-present, all-knowing, and all-powerful to carry on and complete the good work which he has begun in accordance with the free covenant and the counsel of the Three in One regarding those who are the objects of the primal love. O for the privilege of being one of their number.
>
> Dear sister, I feel a degree of thirst to grow up more in the belief in the personal indwelling of the Holy Spirit in my life; and this by way of revelation, not of imagination, as if I thought to comprehend in what way or by what means it happens, which is real idolatry.

This is not the place to discuss the profound theological intuition contained in this passage, the way in which Ann has expressed in a single sentence the tendency, common to both main Christian traditions in the West, to reduce the work of the Holy Spirit to a subsidiary element in the Christian scheme of things. But we should perhaps notice the way in which she, whose imagination was evidently so strong, disclaims the use of her imagination. She is so sure that what she sees is not something of her own creation, which she could fully comprehend, but something which has been revealed to her, which she has been given. She wants to look beyond all images and all imaginings into the mystery of God himself. And we cannot help remarking on the depth of feeling revealed ('I feel my mind being seized by shame . . .') over what many would consider a purely intellectual error of an abstract and remote kind. For Ann everything which touches on Christian doctrine, and above all on the doctrines of the Trinity and the Incarnation, touches immediately the deepest things of her own life and experience, the way of salvation by which, she believes, a door is opened to her into a realm of everlasting truth and joy. Here as always, she speaks of God as if in his presence. She treats of the divine mysteries as of things into which she is already entering, and into which she longs with all her being to enter further.

Indeed the overwhelming impression which the letters convey is of one who is always pushing on, penetrating further into the apprehension of these things. It is the same movement that we find in the hymns; in one she cries,

> O am gael ffydd i edrych
> Gyda'r angylion fry
> Ar drefn yr iechydwriaeth
> Dirgelwch ynddi sy;

(O to have faith to look with the angels above, into the plan of salvation, the mystery that is in it;)

in another

> O am dreiddio i'r adnabyddiaeth
> O'r unig wir a'r bywiol Dduw,
> I'r fath raddau a fo'n lladdfa
> I ddychmygion o bob rhyw;

(O to penetrate to the knowledge of the one true and living God, to such a degree as might be death to imaginings of every kind;)

—

Like all the great Christian mystics she seeks to penetrate beyond all God's gifts to arrive at the Giver himself.

I thought that we have to pass beyond brethren and graces, and love the Giver above the gifts . . . It occurred to me that I should be content to give all that I possess, be it good or bad, to possess the Son, in a marriage union . . . O to be at the feet of our good God as long as we are in the world.

God comes out from himself, from the unapproachable glory of his transcendence, into his creation to give himself to man, to make himself accessible to man's knowledge and man's love. What can his creature do but respond with a similar movement of ecstatic love, coming out from himself, from his own small world of ideas and imaginations into the infinite greatness revealed in God's plan of salvation, in his suffering love? Ann speaks of this in a paragraph of one of her letters where again we see very clearly that the writer of the hymns and the writer of the letters are one and the same person; that her power of handling images does not desert her when she takes to prose. Here as in other places she is interpreting the Old Testament through the prism of the New, so that the figure of King Solomon immediately suggests to her the figure of the Christ, in whom all that Solomon stood for is summed up and fulfilled.

> That word is on my mind tonight, 'Go forth, O ye daughters of Zion, and behold king Solomon with the crown wherewith his mother crowned him in the day of his espousals, and in the day of the gladness of his heart.' I think there is a high and peculiar calling for all who have part in the covenant to leave their own ceiled houses to see their King wearing the crown of thorns and the purple robe. No wonder the sun hid its rays when its Creator was pierced by nails. It is a marvel to me to think who it is that was on the cross, he whose eyes are as a flame of fire piercing through heaven and earth in a single glance, unable to see his creatures, the work of his hands. My mind is too overwhelmed to say anything more on the matter.

As we read on in the letters so we find that the urgency of the desire to abide with God, to give all glory to him, increases.

> I should heartily wish to give all the praise to God the Word, simply for leading me and upholding me so far, and that what remains of my life might be spent in continual communion with God in his Son, because I never can glorify him more than, or so much as by believing in and accepting his Son. Heaven help me to do this, not for my own pleasure alone, but out of reverence for him.

Her whole thought and desire is centred upon God; it is his glory, his praise which always comes first; the salvation of man follows from it, but only as a consequence. It is this very fact which makes her so grieved over the discovery of her own inconstancy.

I am strongly bound to speak the praises of God, and to be grateful to him for some degree of sharing in the fellowship of the mystery. But here is my trouble – failing to abide – continually departing. O for help to abide.

Thomas Charles after long conversation with Ann on spiritual matters is reputed to have told her that one of three things could happen to her. Either she would die young, or she would suffer greatly, or she would become a back-slider. Evidently he felt that such intensity of spiritual vision and desire could hardly be maintained without some great cost. 'No man can see God and live.' When he mentioned the last possibility to her, she wept. The first one was frequently in her mind. Seeing things so much in the light of eternity, believing with such conviction that she was travelling towards that eternal realm, she inevitably thought much about the transitoriness of earthly things, not least her own life. Her last three letters are all signed with similar formulas: 'This from your loving sister, swiftly journeying through a world of time to the great world which lasts for ever.'

There is a feeling of haste about her, as of one for whom things are pressing. But her meditation on death, again a normal part of the traditional Christian way of life, does not take the form of a wish for death in itself. What she longs for is the steadfastness, the freedom from all that deflects her from God which, she believes, she will only find beyond that final frontier.

She herself puts the matter with her customary lucidity and balance:

> Dear sister, I see more need than ever to spend my remaining days in giving myself up daily and continually, body and soul, into the care of him who is able to keep that which is committed unto him against that day. Not to give myself once, but to live continually giving myself, right up to and in the very moment when I put away this tabernacle. Dear sister, the thought of putting it away is particularly sweet sometimes. I can say that this is what cheers me more than anything else in these days, not death itself, but the great gain that is to be got through it. To be able to leave behind every inclination counter to the will of God, to leave behind every capacity to dishonour the law of God, all weakness swallowed up by strength, to become fully conformed to the law which is already on one's heart and to enjoy God's likeness for ever. Dear sister, I am sometimes absorbed so far into these things, that

I completely fail to stand in the way of my duty with regard to temporal things, but I look for a time when I may find release and be with Christ, for that is very much better, although it is very good here through a lattice, and the Lord sometimes reveals through a glass, darkly, as much of his glory as my weak faculties can bear.

It is not surprising in the light of such avowals as these, that some have been led to ask questions about Ann's marriage. How can it be that one who declares herself so wholly given to God, can yet give herself to another in Christian marriage? Again, why is it, if she had to marry, that she did not marry John Hughes, with whom she evidently had so much in common? On the second and relatively minor question, I find the contention of Saunders Lewis wholly convincing. There was too great a social gap between the farmer's daughter and the weaver's apprentice for marriage to have been thinkable. John married Ruth Evans, Ann's maid and companion, and Ann was a witness at their wedding. As to the major question why Ann should have married at all, we may well reply with another question; what else was she to do? Once her father was dead it was evidently difficult for her to maintain the farm at Dolwar with only her brother's help. Every consideration of duty, social, domestic and religious alike, would have suggested that marriage was the right course to take.

We need not disguise from ourselves the thought that had Ann lived in another time or another place, in Wales in the fourteenth century, or in France or Russia in the nineteenth, for instance, she would very possibly have found her place within a monastic community. The kind of contemplative nature which was hers could easily have found its fulfilment within the life of a community wholly given to the work of prayer and praise. Indeed, when her writing is introduced into such a milieu there is an immediate sense of kinship and recognition, as though she had come home. But in her own time such possibility was in no way open to her. If such a way of life was known of at all in the circles in which she moved, it was known entirely at second hand, as a dangerous piece of superstitious and papistical error.

Marriage then would have presented itself to her as a duty. And why should it not also have presented itself as more? We have, it is true, no direct evidence one way or the other. We do not know

40

exactly what were her feelings towards Thomas Griffiths of Meifod; but what little we know of him suggests that he was an eminently lovable man. Once we grant the overriding nature of the commitment to the love of God which is hers, we can surely allow the possibility that while no human love should displace it, a human love may well be compatible with it. On this subject we may hear an eminent and by no means radical Dominican scholar, Fr Festugière. He writes out of the heart of that Christian tradition which has most taken for granted the importance of a life of celibacy for anyone who wishes to give himself wholly to God. He is speaking here of George Herbert, but almost everything that he says could apply equally well to Ann.

> As to knowing whether a *total* offering of oneself to God can be reconciled with a marriage for *love*, I leave it to God to judge. Certainly a sentence like 'he declared his resolution *both* to marry and to enter into the Sacred Order of Priesthood', has something surprising in it for the Catholic reader, at least down till today. But all ways are good and God is truly Lord and All. Herbert's friend, Nicholas Ferrar, refused an offer of marriage, asked to be ordained deacon and kept a voluntary celibacy; his two nieces, Mary and Anna Collett, made a private vow of virginity. Both Herbert and Ferrar left behind a reputation of holiness. And in any case, two facts are to be noted. (1) In the whole collection of The Temple, there is not a single poem relating to human love, (2) it is impossible to read this work without receiving the impression that Herbert was entirely given to God.

These latter points are in every way as true of Ann as of George Herbert. To suggest, as has been done, that her hymn-writing resulted from a disappointment in love, or that it ceased at the time of her marriage (both suppositions for which there is absolutely no evidence) argues a curious lack of sensitivity to the difference of quality between human and divine love. What is characteristic of Ann's writing, in hymns and letters alike, is that it reveals a love of a strangely metaphysical character, a thirsting after eternity, a longing to be taken up into union with the source of life and all existence. It is a longing in which love and knowledge are fused together into one in a single movement of intense desire. There is something almost frightening in it. It is no wonder that, like Herbert and Ferrar before her, she should have left behind her a reputation for holiness, and that she should have been widely recognized as a 'saint', as nearly 'canonized' in that position as is possible in the Protestant tradition to which she belonged.

VI

In view of the extreme narrowness of the external circumstances in which Ann's life was lived it is one of the paradoxes of her work that her hymns and letters can convey such a sense of openness – that man's way is open, he is not shut in, confined within a universe of space and time, whose ultimate boundary is that of death. Indeed it is this quality which is liable to make the reader feel a sense of personal indebtedness towards her, even if he is not able to see 'the plan of salvation' precisely as she sees it. Her writing communicates an extraordinarily powerful sense that human life can find its fulfil-ment, that all the ways are open before man into the kingdom of eternity.

> O'm blaen mi wela ddrws agored,
> A modd i hollol gario'r ma's,
> Yng ngrym y rhoddion a dderbyniodd
> Yr hwn gymerodd agwedd gwas;

(Before me I see an open door, and a way of wholly winning the day, in the strength of the gifts which he received who took the form of a servant;)

Through the power of Christ's triumph over death through death, she is able to say

> Mae'r tywysogaethau wedi eu hyspeilio,
> A'r awdurdodau, ganddo ynghyd,
> A'r carcharwr yn y carchar . . .
>
> Pan esgynodd'r hwn ddisgynodd,
> Gwedi gorffen yma'r gwaith,
> Y pyrth oedd yn dyrchafu eu pennau,
> Dan orfoleddu yn ei hiaith;
> Dorau'n agor, côr yn bywio.
> I Dduw mewn cnawd yr ochor draw,

43

(The principalities have been despoiled, and the powers, yea, all of them, by him, and the gaoler is in the gaol.

When he ascended who had descended, after finishing the work here, the gates were lifting up their heads, exulting in their language; doors were opening, a choir awakening to life, for God in flesh on yonder side,)

Doors were opening. Through the substance of our daily life a way is opened into eternity. There can be for man no final despair.

This theme of the open door finds expression in other hymns in terms of the boldness and freedom of access to God which the believer has in Jesus Christ.

> Myfi a anturiaf yno yn eon,
>> Teyrnwialen aur sydd yn ei law,
> A hon senter at bechadur,
>> Llwyr dderbyniad pawb a ddaw;

(As for me, I will venture thither boldly; it is a golden sceptre he has in his hand, and this pointing straight at the sinner, full acceptance for all who come;)

Here again Ann has identified herself in thought with one of the great figures of the Old Testament, Esther, risking her life on behalf of her people by venturing into the presence of King Ahasuerus, without being bidden. The king holds out his sceptre; all is well, she can go in.

This vision of the way in and the way forward finds its completest statement in the hymn which is totally given up to a meditation on Christ the Way. It is a hymn which, like all the others, is full of biblical allusions, but it is interesting too in that it seems to contain reference to the old Welsh proverb, 'let him that would be head, first be bridge', a proverb, it may be said, which has an extraordinary appositeness to the person of the Christ, as described in the New Testament.

> Ffordd a'i henw yn Rhyfeddol
>> Hen, ac heb heneiddio, yw;
> Ffordd heb ddechreu, eto'n newydd,
>> Ffordd yn gwneud y meirw'n fyw;
> Ffordd i ennill ei thrafaelwyr,
>> Ffordd yn Briod, Ffordd yn Ben,
> Ffordd gysegrwyd, af ar hyddi,
>> I orffwys ynddi draw i'r llen.

(A way whose name is Wonderful, it is old and yet it grows not old; a way without a beginning, yet new, a way that makes the dead alive; a way to win those who travel on it; a way that is a Husband, a way that is a Head, a consecrated way; I shall go along it to rest in it beyond the veil.)

This way into the land of promise is open to us, because already God's image is upon us, and we are made in his likeness. It is this capacity for God, which makes us more and more dissatisfied with the things of earth, taken in themselves, apart from him.

> Mae fy nghalon am ymadael
> A phob rhyw eilunod mwy,
> Am fod arna i'n sgrifenedig
> Ddelw gwrthrych llawer mwy . . .

(My heart would fain depart from every kind of idol henceforth, because inscribed upon me is the likeness of an object far greater . . .)

Indeed this thought of the growing likeness between creature and Creator emboldens Ann to pray in one hymn that her soul may be 'adorned' with the divine likeness,

> Gwna fi'n ddychryn yn dy law,
> I uffern, llygredd, annuwioldeb,
> Wrth edrych arnaf i gael braw;

(Make me a terror in thy hand, that hell, corruption, ungodliness may feel fear at the sight of me;)

Man is being clothed with the attributes of God, is becoming already here by God's gift that which God is by nature.

But of course, in this life we are only setting out on this way. Here the likeness is only revealed in part. So in another hymn she prays,

> O am bara i uchel yfed
> O ffrydiau'r iechydwriaeth fawr,
> Nes fy nghwbwl ddisychedu
> Am ddarfodedig bethau'r llawr;
> Byw dan ddisgwyl am fy Arglwydd
> Bod, pan ddel, yn effro iawn,
> I agoryd iddo'n ebrwydd
> A mwynhau ei ddelw'n llawn.

(O to continue to drink deep of the streams of the great salvation, until I wholly lose the thirst for the passing things of earth; to live watching for my Lord, to be wide awake when he comes, to open to him quickly and enjoy his likeness to the full.)

If we find in these verses an insistence on the passing nature of this world, an emphasis on the necessity of leaving aside all created things which disturbs us, we must surely recognize that this movement away from the earth is far from being purely negative. It is not renunciation for the sake of renunciation. It is because she has seen something else, something which she strains all her powers to convey to us, that she exhorts us to turn aside from finite things which can never wholly satisfy man's heart and mind.

> Rhyfeddu a wna i â mawr ryfeddod
> Pan ddêl i ben y ddedwydd awr
> Caf weld fy meddwl, sy yma'n gwibio
> Ar ôl teganau gwael y llawr,
> Wedi ei dragwyddol setlo
> Ar wrthrych mawr ei berson Ef,
> A diysgog gydymffurfio
> Â phur a sanctaidd ddeddfau'r nef.

(I shall wonder with a great wonder when the blessed hour is fulfilled for me to see my mind, which here wanders after the base toys of earth, eternally settled upon the great object of His person, and unshakeably conformed to the pure and holy laws of heaven.)

> Melys gofio y cyfamod
> Draw a wnaed gan Dri yn Un,
> Tragwyddol syllu ar y person
> A gymerodd natur dyn; . . .
>
> Byw heb wres na haul yn taro,
> Byw heb allu marw mwy, . . .
> Nofio'n afon bur y bywyd,
> Diderfyn heddwch sanctaidd Dri,
> Dan d'wniadau digymylau
> Gwerthfawr [angau] Calfari.

(Sweet it is to remember the Covenant that was made yonder by Three in One, to gaze eternally upon the person who took the nature of man . . .

To live without stroke of heat or sun, to live unable to die any more
. . . to swim in the pure river of life, the endless peace of the holy Three,
under the cloudless rays of the precious death on Calvary.)

There is in any life which is marked by a peculiar genius, a capacity
to sum up and express the life of a great multitude of people. A
statesman who speaks for his nation in its time of need may do it in
one way, a great artist in another. But in a life whose significance and
intention is explicitly religious, this can happen in a particularly
universal way. For here there is a wrestling with the ultimate questions
of man's life. Is there a way along which he may go? Is it a way which
leads to any goal, or is it doomed to end in futility? Here the final
questions of meaning and meaninglessness are constantly and
directly confronted.

In the case of Ann, we have a woman in whose life the things of
many ages and of many peoples come together into one. The great
abiding images of the Bible come to new life. The central affirmations
of Christian faith, that God becomes man so that man may enter
into that communion of life and love which is in God, find new and
powerful expression. As has already been said, she stands at the
centre of the Christian tradition of prayer and faith and despite the
limitations of her work, her stature is to be measured against the
great and unquestioned figures of the Church's history, a St Theresa
of Avila or a Julian of Norwich, a St Symeon the New Theologian,
or a St Seraphim of Sarov. But this place which is hers within the
universal chorus of the Church's praise, in no way cuts her off from
her own people, from the nation which gave her birth. For it is the
characteristic of holiness, the life of God, that when it touches the
things of earth it destroys separations without destroying distinctions.
It creates harmony and peace without eliminating diversity and
richness. So it is that Ann stands within the long tradition of prayer
and of the praise of God which first burst out in Wales in the age of
saints, which ran as a kind of bass line under the exuberant counter-
point of the poetry of the middle ages, to break out again in the
apparently unpropitious circumstances of the late eighteenth
century. Here in the Berwyns at a moment when in Europe the
meaning of this tradition was largely being forgotten, a life was lived
in the light of eternity, 'swiftly travelling through the world of time
to the great world which lasts for ever'. It was a life in which the

things of earth were constantly mingled with the things of heaven, in which the joy which can light up man's life below, was constantly associated with the rejoicing of the angelic powers. It was in itself a point of intersection of the timeless with time, a place where the narrowness of this world opens out onto the spaces of the great world which lasts for ever. As R. S. Thomas puts it in his poem 'Fugue for Ann Griffiths'

> Here for a few years
> the spirit sang on a bone bough
> at eternity's window, the flesh trembling
> at the splendour of a forgiveness
> too impossible to believe in, yet believing

There is much here which we may feel that we do not understand, much that eludes our comprehension or our belief. But what we do see, whether it be little or whether it be much, is something that gives grounds for hope, grounds for faith, grounds for love, in a world which knows itself to be desperately in need of these things.

A Note on Further Reading

In English:

Homage to Ann Griffiths (Church in Wales Publications, 1976). This contains a verse translation of the hymns and a notable lecture on Ann by Saunders Lewis, together with an introduction by H.A. Hodges.

John Ryan, (ed.), *The Hymns of Ann Griffiths* (Tŷ ar y Graig, 1980). The text in Welsh with a translation, and a critical introduction.

A. M. Allchin, 'Ann Griffiths, Mystic and Theologian' in *The Kingdom of Love and Knowledge* (Darton, Longman & Todd, 1979).

In Welsh:

Sian Megan, (ed.), *Gwaith Ann Griffiths* (Christopher Davies, 1982). A critical edition of the hymns and letters, with a full introduction.

Dyfnallt Morgan, (ed.), *Y Ferch o Dolwar Fach* (Gwasg Gwynedd, 1977). Lectures given at the 1976 summer school on Ann.

R. M. Jones, *Ann Griffiths, Y Cyfrinydd Sylweddol* (Llyfrgell Efengylaidd Cymru, 1977). An essay on Ann's teaching by a noted evangelical scholar.